# BASEBALL LEGENDS

Hank Aaron

Grover Cleveland Alexander

Ernie Banks

Albert Belle

Johnny Bench

Yogi Berra

Barry Bonds

Roy Campanella

Roger Clemens

Roberto Clemente

Ty Cobb

Dizzy Dean

Joe DiMaggio

Bob Feller

Lou Gehrig

Bob Gibson

Ken Griffey, Jr.

Rogers Hornsby

Randy Johnson

Walter Johnson

Chipper Jones

Sandy Koufax

Life in the Minor Leagues

Greg Maddux

Mickey Mantle

Christy Mathewson

Willie Mays

Mark McGwire

Stan Musial

Mike Piazza

Cal Ripken, Jr.

Brooks Robinson

Frank Robinson

Jackie Robinson

Pete Rose

Babe Ruth

Nolan Ryan

Mike Schmidt

Tom Seaver

Duke Snider

Warren Spahn

Casey Stengel

Frank Thomas

Honus Wagner

Larry Walker

Ted Williams

Carl Yastrzemski

Cy Young

CHELSEA HOUSE PUBLISHERS

# ROGER CLEMENS

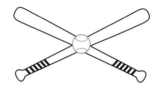

*Norman L. Macht*

*Introduction by*
*Jim Murray*

---

*Senior Consultant*
*Earl Weaver*

## CHELSEA HOUSE PUBLISHERS
*Philadelphia*

**Produced by Choptank Syndicate, Inc.**

*Editor and Picture Researcher:* Norman L. Macht
*Production Coordinator and Editorial Assistant:* Mary E. Hull
*Design and Production:* Lisa Hochstein

CHELSEA HOUSE PUBLISHERS

Editor in Chief: Stephen Reginald
Managing Editor: James Gallagher
Production Manager: Pamela Loos
Art Director: Sara Davis
Director of Photography: Judy L. Hasday
Senior Production Editor: Lisa Chippendale
Publishing Coordinator: James McAvoy
Cover Design and Digital Illustration: Keith Trego

Cover Photos: Front: action shot, AP/Wide World Photos; portrait, courtesy Toronto
Blue Jays
Back: AP/Wide World Photos

The Chelsea House World Wide Web site
address is http://www.chelseahouse.com

First Printing

1 3 5 7 9 8 6 4 2

Library of Congress Cataloging-in-Publication Data

Macht, Norman L. (Norman Lee), 1929-
    Roger Clemens / Norman L. Macht; introduction by Jim Murray
        64 p.    cm.— (Baseball legends)
    Includes bibliographical references (p. 61) and index.
    Summary: A biography of the pitcher for the Toronto Blue Jays who
won his fourth Cy Young award in 1997.
    ISBN 0-7910-5156-0 (hc)
    1. Clemens, Roger—Juvenile literature. 2. Baseball players—United States—
Biography—Juvenile literature. 3. Pitchers (Baseball)—United States—
Biography—Juvenile literature.
[1. Clemens, Roger. 2. Baseball players.] I. Title. II. Series.
GV865.C44M33  1999
796.357'092— dc21
[B]                                                          98-51064
                                                                CIP
                                                                AC

T   100419

# CONTENTS

# What Makes a Star

### *Jim Murray*

No one has ever been able to explain to me the mysterious alchemy that makes one man a .350 hitter and another player, more or less identical in physical makeup, hard put to hit .200. You look at an Al Kaline, who played with the Detroit Tigers from 1953 to 1974. He was pale, stringy, almost poetic-looking. He always seemed to be struggling against a bad case of mononucleosis. But with a bat in his hands, he was King Kong. During his career, he hit 399 home runs, rapped out 3,007 hits, and compiled a .297 batting average.

Form isn't the reason. The first time anybody saw Roberto Clemente step into the batter's box for the Pittsburgh Pirates, the best guess was that Clemente would be back in Double A ball in a week. He had one foot in the bucket and held his bat at an awkward angle—he looked as though he couldn't hit an outside pitch. A lot of other ballplayers may have had a better-looking stance. Yet they never led the National League in hitting in four different years, the way Clemente did.

Not every ballplayer is born with the ability to hit a curveball. Nor is exceptional hand-eye coordination the key to heavy hitting. Big league locker rooms are filled with players who have all the attributes, save one: discipline. Every baseball man can tell you a story about a pitcher who throws a ball faster than anyone has ever seen but who has no control on or *off* the field.

The Hall of Fame is full of people who transformed themselves into great ballplayers by working at the sport, by studying the game, and making sacrifices. They're overachievers—and winners. If you want to find them, just watch the World Series. Or simply read about New York Yankee great Lou Gehrig; Ted Williams, "the Splendid Splinter" of the Boston Red Sox; or the Dodgers' strikeout king, Sandy Koufax.

A pitcher *should* be able to win a lot of ballgames with a 98-miles-per-hour fastball. But what about the pitcher who wins 20 games a year with a fastball so slow that you can catch it with your teeth? Bob Feller of the Cleveland Indians got into the Hall of Fame with a blazing fastball that glowed in the dark. National League star Grover Cleveland Alexander got there with a pitch that took considerably longer to reach the plate; but when it did arrive, the pitch was exactly where Alexander wanted it to be—and the last place the batter expected it to be.

There are probably more players with exceptional ability who didn't make it to the major leagues than there are who did. A number of great hitters, bored with fielding practice, had to be dropped from their team because their home-run production didn't make up for their lapses in the field. And then there are players like Brooks Robinson of the Baltimore Orioles, who made himself into a human vacuum cleaner at third base because he knew that working hard to become an expert fielder would win him a job in the big leagues.

A star is not something that flashes through the sky. That's a comet. Or a meteor. A star is something you can steer ships by. It stays in place and gives off a steady glow; it is fixed, permanent. A star works at being a star.

And that's how you tell a star in baseball. He shows up night after night and takes pride in how brightly he shines. He's Willie Mays running so hard his hat keeps falling off; Ty Cobb sliding to stretch a single into a double; Lou Gehrig, after being fooled in his first two at-bats, belting the next pitch off the light tower because he's taken the time to study the pitcher. Stars never take themselves for granted. That's why they're stars.

# 1

# GOING FOR THE RECORD

**R**oger "The Rocket" Clemens was zeroed in like a laser beam on a special mission as he took the mound at Tiger Stadium for the Boston Red Sox on the night of September 18, 1996. His game face, always a picture of intense concentration, looked even more menacing than usual. He glared at the first batter like a warrior facing an evil foe.

His mission: to match the record of the great Cy Young, whose name was on the award Clemens had won three times. Young had pitched for Boston 90 years earlier, winning 192 of his record 511 games in a Red Sox uniform. Thirty-eight of those wins had been shutouts.

No Boston pitcher had ever matched Young's Red Sox marks. Now Clemens was one win and one shutout away from tying them. He wanted those records. With maybe two more starts remaining, and the likelihood that he would be leaving Boston after the season, he let manager Kevin Kennedy know what his goals were that night.

He asked a favor of Kennedy: "If it's the late innings and there's a runner on third and less than two outs, can we play the infield in?" That would give them a better chance to throw out the

*While going for one record, Roger Clemens tied another one when he struck out 20 Detroit Tigers on September 18, 1996, in Detroit. Here he pumps his fist after making Travis Fryman his 20th punchout.*

runner on a ground ball. Recognizing that Clemens had carried the team for the last 10 years, Kennedy agreed. They owed him every chance at the record.

"We went over the lineup as usual," catcher Bill Haselman recalled. "It took 10 minutes at most. Warming up didn't seem any different from any other game. He's always focused and prepared and knows what he has to do that day. He was focused on the Cy Young Boston records, not strikeouts that night."

The whole team knew what Roger was after and supported him. Shortstop Nomar Garciaparra said, "His intensity on the mound raised the intensity level of everybody playing behind him. You wanted to dive to make every play you could for him. If he was going for a shutout you wanted to do whatever you could to keep it going."

They didn't have to.

It was evident from the first pitch that Clemens had keyed himself up to some superhuman level. Home plate umpire Tim McClelland said, "I've never seen a pitcher so dominant. He threw a two-seam fastball, four-seam fastball, forkball, breaking ball, and changeup and he threw them all right where he wanted to. Nobody ever knew what was coming. He was throwing a great forkball, fastball at the knees, and he threw the forkball in the same place and they thought it was a fastball and they were swinging at it as it broke down in the dirt. The hitters were just shaking their heads."

Catcher Bill Haselman observed, "He had outstanding velocity but he mixed in other pitches that kept the hitters off balance. Big league hitters will eventually catch up with it if you throw nothing but fastballs.

"His split-finger or forkball was just dropping right off the table."

The Red Sox scored three in the fourth; two runs came in on a single by Haselman, which he later could not recall. "I was concentrating so much on working with him for that win and shutout I didn't remember anything else."

From the fourth inning on, the 8,799 Detroit fans started cheering for Clemens, too. Roger struck out the side in the second, the fifth, and the sixth innings. He wasn't counting the Ks (strikeouts); he was just after that shutout. But the players on the bench were counting.

*The award for the best pitcher of the year in each league is named for Cy Young, who won 511 games over 22 years from 1890 to 1911. Young pitched for the Red Sox in the first World Series game ever played, in 1903. He won two games as Boston won the Series.*

Whenever the Red Sox batted, Clemens went into the clubhouse to stretch and avoid the distractions of the crowded dugout. When they came off the field after the eighth inning, leading 4–0, somebody told Haselman that Clemens had 19 strikeouts, just one away from the record. Surprised, the catcher wondered if he should tell Clemens, so they could go after 21. "But he was cruising along so well, I decided not to tell him. I didn't want to have him focus on something like that, instead of his original goal."

Strikeouts take a lot of pitches, but nobody even thought about taking Clemens out of the game. Later, his pitch count having reached 151 for the night, he said, "When you're chasing the guy they named the pitching award for, boy, you don't get tired."

In the ninth the first Tiger batter, Alan Trammell, popped up. Ruben Sierra then singled for the fourth Detroit hit. Tony Clark hit a fly ball for out number two. Then Clemens struck out Travis Fryman for the fourth time to end the game.

Haselman was the first to reach the mound. "You know what you just did, right?" he asked Roger.

"Yeah, I got the win and the shutout."

"You struck out 20," Haselman said.

Not only had Clemens tied Cy Young's Red Sox records, he had also tied the record for strikeouts. The only pitcher who had ever done that was—Clemens himself, 10 years earlier. (In 1998 the Cubs' Kerry Wood also struck out 20 in a game.)

Clemens had two more starts to beat Cy Young's records. On September 23, he started against the Yankees' Andy Pettitte, who had played for San Jacinto Junior College 10 years after Clemens. He went seven innings against the Yankees, gave up one run on five hits, but left with the score 1–1. He was still firing in the mid-90s and had struck out eight, but he admitted, "I was gassed. I'd thrown a lot of bullets the last two games. My legs were spent."

He lost his last start, also against the Yankees, 4–2.

Discussing his two 20-strikeout games, Clemens said, "It made me the most proud that I didn't walk a single hitter in either of those games. . . . I'm a power pitcher, a pitcher, not a thrower."

# 2

# "LOVE THOSE PUNCHOUTS"

**W**illiam Roger Clemens was born on August 4, 1962, in Dayton, Ohio. He was named for his father, Bill, whom he never really knew; five months later his mother, Bess, left her husband and took her five children with her: Rick, Randy, Brenda, Janet, and little Bill. As soon as he could, Bill let everybody know that he preferred to be called Roger.

Their father had discouraged his athletic sons from playing sports. But their mother encouraged them, saving up premium stamps to get Randy, a star baseball and basketball player, his first glove.

The family's lives changed dramatically when Bess married Woody Booher, a tool and die maker, and they moved to Vandalia, a small town of 6,000 in western Ohio. They had a big house with a huge yard, a swimming pool, and a barn with six horses. Roger lived in a world of motorcycles and horseback riding. He had a BB gun and covered miles of trails on his dirt bike. Woody took the kids on his motorcycle, Roger in front and one of his sisters on the back. Roger's mother had her own

*Spring Woods baseball coach Charles Maiorana (left) and Neal Stephenson of his 1998 team pose in front of the scoreboard honoring their most famous graduate. During the winter Clemens sometimes joins the high school players when they tie a tire to a 15-foot rope and harness around their shoulders and pull it while sprinting.*

Honda. They went on buggy rides and traveled as far west as the Grand Canyon on vacations.

Roger's grandmother, Myrta Lee, lived nearby and was the disciplinarian of the family. When somebody got into mischief, she ordered them to break off a branch of a tree and bring it to her. Then she'd use the switch on them. Roger soon learned to bring in the smallest branch he could find.

When Roger was four, another sister, Bonnie, was born. Two years later Rick was drafted into the army and went off to fight in Vietnam.

Roger's idyllic childhood suddenly ended when he was nine. One evening Woody got up from the dinner table feeling ill. Roger and his little sister did not know what was happening when they peered out of a basement window and saw the red lights of an ambulance outside the house. Later they were told that Woody had died of a heart attack.

The close-knit family grew even more together. Their mother worked three jobs, stocking coolers and cleaning buildings, and somehow found the time to go to their ball games.

"I grew up extremely fast," Roger said. "Watching my mother work the way she did to make sure I had whatever first-rate equipment I needed probably is what gave me my work ethic and drive and determination."

Randy, by now an all-state athlete at Vandalia High School, was Roger's hero, mentor, and protector. He encouraged Roger's love for baseball, made him the school team's batboy, and talked a Little League coach into letting his eight-year-old brother pitch.

Big for his age, Roger could throw harder than boys a few years older. He was also blessed with near-perfect control. But throwing strikes to 12-year-olds at first got him lit up. "You'll never be as good as your brother Randy," the hitters taunted him.

That's when Roger's "I'll show you" attitude was born. It never left him. He turned his speed up a notch and began striking out those bigger hitters. One day his mother watched him strike out three hitters in a row on nine pitches, each fastball cracking into the catcher's mitt like a rifle shot. When she rode him home on her Honda, she told the family she knew they had something special in Roger.

By the time he was 10 he was working on his plan to be a big league ballplayer. "I always knew what I could do if I got the chance to do it," he said. "I thought other kids played ahead of me when I was better than they were. I had to sit."

At 13 Roger was almost six feet tall and weighed 185 pounds. He was mowing down 16-year-old hitters in the spring and running backs in the fall as a defensive lineman on the football team. Later, when he gave up football, he missed the aggressive contact, and never lost what he called "that football mentality."

The next year the family moved to a suburb of Houston, Texas, where Roger's brothers, Randy and Rick, already lived. Roger enjoyed going to the Astrodome and sitting near the bullpen where he could watch the pitchers. Nolan Ryan and Tom Seaver were his models: workhorses with strong legs and muscular thighs. He dreamed of emulating them, and having his picture on the cover of *Sports Illustrated*.

As a sophomore at Dulles High School, Roger pitched and played first base. He grew to 6'2" and 220 pounds. He was throwing at about 75 miles an hour, and won 12 games against only one loss. But Randy was not impressed. "You need better coaching and tougher competition," he told his brother.

So Bess moved the family across town to Katy and Roger enrolled at Spring Woods High. The school coach, Charlie Maiorana, stressed discipline and conditioning, lessons the young Clemens took to heart. "He was self-motivated, driven to reach his goals," the coach recalled. "When it got dark we had to tell him to go home."

Every day Roger ran the two miles home carrying a knapsack full of books on his back. He watched his diet and kept a journal that helped him determine the eating and sleeping patterns and weight at which he pitched his best. He studied books and films on pitching mechanics, and stood in front of a mirror practicing his throwing motion and move to first base. He continued to do these things throughout his career.

*Coach Charlie Maiorana taught the young Roger Clemens that mental and physical preparation were the keys to success. He also encouraged Clemens not to back down to anybody.*

"He learned that preparation is all important," coach Maiorana said. "Nothing can happen unless you're prepared for it mentally and physically. The other thing I stressed was, 'Don't back down to anybody.'"

Being born in August enabled Roger to start each season in younger leagues, then play for older teams the same summer. In 1979 he played up to 10 games a week in three leagues. His American Legion team won the state championship.

"People think of Roger as a pitcher," Maiorana said, "but he was also a top first baseman. He batted fourth in the lineup and was among the home run leaders."

Roger also learned that he had a high tolerance of pain. Once he flipped a weight bench while working out and almost lost an eye. His nose was broken several times on the football field, and he played the second half of a game with a broken ankle.

Roger had a 13–5 record in his senior year, but his fastball topped out at 85. Big league scouts paid little attention to pitchers who could not throw any harder than that, despite a good curve and precise control. "I was just the reverse of Nolan Ryan," Roger recalled, "who could turn it loose but had no idea where it was going."

No big league bonuses or college scholarships awaited him. But he had impressed coach Wayne Graham of nearby San Jacinto Junior College. Graham loved pitchers who could throw strikes, and that was Roger's strong point.

Roger went to San Jacinto, where Graham drove him hard, hollering at him when he made mistakes. Clemens thrived under the demanding taskmaster. He grew to 6'4" and broke 90 with

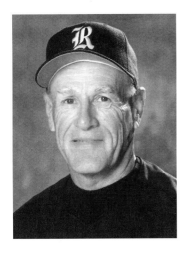

*When Roger Clemens graduated from high school, only Wayne Graham of San Jacinto Junior College offered him a chance to play college ball. Under Graham's hard-driving leadership, Clemens became a power pitcher.*

his fastball for the first time. He loved to win; he also caught K fever. "Love those punchouts," he said.

Roger was now a power pitcher with control, and scouts took notice. The New York Mets invited him to a tryout at the Astrodome when they were in Houston. He was on the same field where he had watched Nolan Ryan pop catcher's mitts with his fastballs. The Mets offered him a $25,000 signing bonus. Roger turned it down.

Like many Texas athletes, Roger wanted to play for legendary coach Cliff Gustafson at the University of Texas. Gustafson's teams had gone to the College World Series more than any other school. Their motto was: "The Texas tradition will not be entrusted to the timid or the weak."

Texas offered Roger a scholarship, but making the Longhorns team was not easy. Nine players on the 1982 team would be drafted by major league clubs. The competition brought out the best in Roger; he was 15–2 as a sophomore before losing the College World Series final to Miami, 2–1.

The Longhorns were picked Number 1 in the country in 1983. Crowds of scouts followed them. Roger saw 40 radar guns focused on every pitch he threw. He had some rough outings; starting and relieving wore him down. His temper exploded after he was knocked out of one game. These things caused scouts to downgrade him. They turned their attention to other Longhorns whose stats were better.

But one Boston scout, Danny Doyle, saw something beyond the stats. He urged the Red Sox to draft Roger "for his determination and heart."

"Roger had a heart as big as the United States," said veteran Boston scout Broadway

Charlie Wagner. "He was the most devoted to his business of any kid we ever saw. Some guys have the stuff but they just coast and don't work at it. He wanted the ball and would not let you down."

In the College World Series Texas needed a win over Alabama to clinch the championship. Roger had a 4–3 lead in the ninth when Alabama's Dave Magadan led off with a double. Gustafson went out to the mound to take the ball from Roger. "I ain't coming out," Roger said. "I want this one." He got it.

Roger and several of his teammates expected to go high in the first round of the major league draft. Both Roger and the Red Sox were surprised to find him still available after 18 players had been taken. At Doyle's insistence they picked him. Roger signed with the Red Sox for $121,000 and was assigned to Winter Haven in the Class A Florida State League.

# 3

## ROGER AGAINST THE WORLD

**L**ike many college stars who are used to near-major league clubhouses, stadiums, and crowds, Roger Clemens was shocked by life in the low minor leagues. "There were 50 people in the stands, tops," he wrote in *Rocket Man.* "There were bugs everywhere. It rained every day. One night [the first baseman] almost got hit in the head with a fish. A bird had plucked it out of Lake Lulu and was carrying it back to its nest atop one of the towers in center field. The bird couldn't make it, let go, and it just missed [the player's] head at first base."

Clemens couldn't wait to get out of there. "Traveling on a bus eight or nine hours making $800 a month wasn't my idea of playing professional baseball."

Disappointed by the light workouts assigned by the manager, Roger trained on his own, running two or three miles a day while the other pitchers did a few outfield sprints. "In the minor leagues I passed a lot of kids who definitely had more talent than I did. But they never made it. I felt that some of them couldn't distinguish between the time to play and the time to do their work. Some of them were satisfied just telling people around town that they were a professional ballplayer."

Roger won three of his four starts, striking out 36 and not walking a batter. Then he was promoted to New Britain in the AA Eastern League. There he was 4–1 in seven starts, blanking the Lynn Pirates on three hits in the playoff finals. Since the spring he had pitched 298 innings, won 26 games, and celebrated two championships. But all that paled when the Red Sox invited him to Boston to work out with the team during the last few weeks of the 1983 season.

Since junior college Roger had worn the number 21, and it was considered the family's lucky number. When he walked into the Boston clubhouse he found a new white uniform with his name and a big red 21 on the back. Luckily no other Boston regular wanted the number. As soon as he could, Roger got a SOX-21 license plate for his car.

Roger believed he would make the big team in 1984, but they sent him down to Pawtucket in the AAA International League. He had a 2–3 record when they called him up to Boston on May 11. Four days later he made his big league debut in Cleveland. He was nervous and his control deserted him. He grooved too many fastballs and was shelled. His next start was better; he earned his first big league win, 5–4, at Minnesota.

Clemens struggled at first, but his catcher, Jeff Newman, was impressed. "On the mound he was total business. He was out there for a reason. You never saw a smile, no joking around on the mound. He was there to learn."

Jerry Remy, in his seventh and last year as the Boston second baseman, said, "Roger was a bull. I had not seen any other young pitcher come to the Red Sox with that air of confidence about them."

One thing Roger learned was that his 96-mph heater could be hit by big league sluggers. Always eager to be challenged by the best, Clemens couldn't wait to face the best longball hitter of the time, Reggie Jackson. He had seen Jackson hit three home runs in a 1977 World Series game on TV. His brother Randy warned him about not getting too carried away if he struck out a big slugger once or twice. "They'll catch up with you," he cautioned Roger.

The big day came. Jackson was with the California Angels. First time up, Jackson fanned on three pitches. Next time up, Clemens punched him out again. The third time, he had two strikes on Jackson, but Reggie smacked the next pitch into the seats for a two-run homer.

Jimy Williams was the Toronto manager when the Blue Jays got their first look at Clemens. Fifteen years later he could still remember "standing in the third base dugout in Fenway and I can hear his arm coming through the air when he's throwing the ball. That's how fast his arm was moving. I could actually hear it in the dugout. Amazing."

The umpires also got their first look at the face of Clemens's fierce combativeness. "When he broke in he was Roger against the world," said umpire Durwood Merrill. "If he didn't like a call, he would give you that stare. An umpire could tell by the way he came off the mound and caught the ball that Roger was not happy."

When Clemens bore down, he gritted his teeth, and had to use a mouthpiece to protect them. He didn't hesitate to pitch inside. If the hitter was intimidated by it, so much the better.

At least 90 percent of baseball is mental. When Roger's fastball got too much of the plate and hitters hammered it, he would lose confidence in it and switch to other pitches. His whole game plan would blow up. Pitching coach Lee Stange tried to tell him, "Just let the ball go. With your stuff and control, you'll win." It was a reminder that Clemens would need to hear more than once.

Beginning with a July 26 shutout of the White Sox, Clemens hit his stride. He won six in a row, including a 15-strikeout, no-walk outing against Kansas City. Then, on August 31, his rookie year came to an abrupt end. He had struck out seven and given up one hit by the fourth inning when his right forearm started to stiffen from a strained tendon. The Red Sox were out of the pennant race, so they took no chances and benched him for the rest of the season.

That fall Clemens did his running and exercises, interrupted only by his marriage to Debbie Godfrey in Houston and a honeymoon in Hawaii. He went to spring training feeling fit.

In 1985 the Red Sox had a new pitching coach, Bill Fischer, who later recalled his first impression of Clemens. "He was a brash, cocky young whippersnapper, a notch above the rest. Throwing on the side he made the catcher's mitt crack, and all eyes focused on him."

Fischer introduced Roger to Tom Seaver, who showed him how to throw a four-seam fastball that would explode up and out of the strike zone, to go with his two-seamer that sank as it crossed the plate. "Roger was very coachable," Fischer said. "It helped him for me to find the right words that would click with him so he would remember them.

"If your hands are too close to your body in the stretch, and your weight goes on your right heel, you will throw high and inside to a right-hand batter. Roger did that sometimes. So I gave him two reminders: 'Go toe to toe,' to keep the weight on his toes, and 'Get the ball out of the glove,' so his arm got up in time to be throwing downhill. If he throws outside, it's lights out for the hitters."

In addition to perfecting Roger's mechanics, Fischer worked on getting him to control his emotions. "He would blow up at himself and throw things, and I tried to calm him down." Once, after Roger banged a door with his right

*"Something people don't understand about pitchers," said Bill Fischer, Clemens's pitching coach with the Red Sox. "They are freaks. Every great pitcher I have ever known is a freak of nature. Roger's only problem is that he works too hard, and sometimes overpitches."*

fist, Fischer reminded him, "You hit a wall with your fist, you could break your hand."

On May 17 in Cleveland, Clemens shut out the Indians, but the cold, damp wind blowing in off Lake Erie left him with a stiff arm. Believing it was just tendinitis, he pitched in pain for a month. But the ache burrowed into his shoulder. Warming up for a game on July 7 at Anaheim, the pain was so sharp and so obvious, Fischer stopped him. Clemens pleaded that he could pitch, but Fischer ordered him to get dressed and go back to Boston for a physical.

Angry and frustrated, Clemens feared that his quest for greatness might be over after just two months. His path from the dugout to the club-house was littered with his torn jersey, loose buttons, kicked-off shoes, a thrown chair, and a door torn off its hinges. He went out to the parking lot and ran through the streets in 90-degree heat until his temper cooled. It didn't help his temper when a Boston newspaper columnist wrote that there was nothing really wrong with Clemens; it was all in his head.

Clemens tried different remedies and exercises, but he continued to pitch in pain. On August 11 at Yankee Stadium he ground out five innings before his delivery became so erratic manager John McNamara took him out.

Further examination revealed that a small piece of cartilage in his shoulder had broken off and was causing the pain. A 20-minute operation removed it. "How you recover now depends entirely on how religiously you work at the rehabilitation," the doctor told him.

The doctor didn't know that, when it came to sticking religiously to a conditioning and exercise program, Roger Clemens was the most devout person in the world.

Throughout the winter of 1985–86 Roger Clemens devoted himself to regaining his pitching strength. He ran every day, did weight squats to build his legs, and exercised with three- and five-pound weights—and nothing heavier. Then he began throwing, not too hard, but without pain.

# ROCKET MAN

Roger Clemens went to spring training in the spring of 1986 feeling no pain, but afraid that his injury and surgery had robbed him of his fastball. In the early games he concentrated on trying to trick hitters rather than punching them out. Bill Fischer tracked his progress on a radar gun. One day he said to Clemens, "You're throwing all breaking stuff. How hard do you think you're throwing your fastball?"

Clemens guessed, "Eighty-four."

Fischer showed him the readings. "Ninety-three."

Clemens's eyes lit up like a Christmas tree.

When the season started, he got off to a rocky start, but Boston bats helped him with his first three starts. On April 29, he faced the Seattle Mariners at Fenway. Clemens began the game by striking out the side. His cutter and slider were sharp; he fanned two more in the second, and eight in a row from the fourth to the sixth.

Seattle catcher Steve Yeager said to home plate umpire Vic Voltaggio, "Vic, this guy's going to do something special tonight. We couldn't hit him with a tennis racquet."

*Smokey Joe Wood won 16 in a row for the Red Sox in 1912, still the American League record, and 34 for the year. He also won three World Series games that year. When Clemens won 14 in a row to start the 1986 season, pitching coach Bill Fischer began calling him Smokey. Fischer still tries to call or fax Clemens whenever Roger wins a game. "I still address him as Smokey," Fischer said, "and when he calls me he says, 'This is Smokey.'"*

The strikeouts kept coming, but neither team scored until Seattle's Gorman Thomas hit a home run in the seventh. Boston's Dwight Evans responded with a three-run homer in the bottom of the seventh to give Clemens a 3–1 lead.

Now Clemens really turned up the heat. He fanned two in the eighth; the K count was up to 18. Clemens had known something was happening because of the fans' reactions, but he was not aware that he was approaching the record of 19 until pitcher Al Nipper mentioned it to him in the clubhouse while the Red Sox batted in the eighth.

Clemens went out for the ninth, still throwing 97 mph. While his teammates in the dugout chanted, "One, two, three—blastoff!" he fanned the first two batters to break the record.

"It was the greatest pitching performance I ever saw," umpire Vic Voltaggio said. "I worked three no-hitters, and never saw a pitcher so dominant. In a no-hitter there are often some great defensive plays and some luck needed to preserve it. Roger needed none of that. The slider got everybody; it was on the black all night."

Roger was as proud that he had not walked a batter as he was of the 20 Ks. The next day somebody put a sign, "Rocket Man," over his locker, and Roger had a new nickname: Rocket.

The Red Sox climbed into first place and Clemens was on a roll. He had won his first 14 decisions. The American League record was 15 wins to start a season, set by Dave McNally of the Orioles. On July 2 Clemens went after the record-tying win against Toronto. He had a 2–1 lead on a one-hitter in the eighth, when the Blue Jays tied it and had runners on second and third. Manager John McNamara brought in a relief pitcher. Clemens watched angrily as the reliever allowed the runners to score. He told the manager he never wanted to come out again with the game on the line.

*Clemens holds up his trophy after being named the Most Valuable Player (MVP) of the 1986 All-Star Game in Houston. He threw three perfect innings as the AL starter in the Astrodome.*

Clemens was picked to start the All-Star Game against the Mets' 1985 Cy Young winner, Doc Gooden. It was a hectic, exciting event for Roger because it was played in the Astrodome. His family and many friends were there. He retired all nine batters he faced on 25 pitches, 21 of them strikes, and was the winning pitcher and MVP in the AL's 3–2 win.

On August 30, exactly one year after his shoulder surgery, Clemens won his 20th. He finished with a league-leading 24–4 and 2.46 ERA. The Red Sox won the AL East.

The playoff against the West winners, the California Angels, was as tense as a stretched rubber band. Entertaining all the family and friends who swarmed into Boston distracted Roger from his usual routine. Completely out of sync, he lost the opener, 8–1. He came back to pitch Game 4 on three days' rest and took a 3–0 lead into the ninth. Then, trying to get the game over quickly, he got careless and threw some fat pitches. The Angels tied it and went on to win in the 11th.

The Red Sox were now down 3 games to 1. The next day California had a 5–2 lead and their champagne iced after eight innings. Clemens went into the clubhouse where he watched on TV with a few other players. Their hopes rose a little when Don Baylor hit a two-run homer in the ninth to make it 5–4.

Ballplayers are superstitious. Clemens insisted that everyone stay in their same seats as the team continued to rally. If anybody moved, Roger screamed at them to stay put. Their caps went into rally formation—inside out. It seemed to work when Dave Henderson hit a two-out, two-strike pitch for a home run to give them a 6–5 lead.

California knotted it in the bottom of the ninth. The Red Sox scored once in the top of the 11th. The rally caps were turned backward, and the Sox lived to play another day.

Back in Fenway they won Game 6, 10–4, and Roger was ready to pitch the decisive game—ready mentally but not physically. He felt as if he had the flu. His legs shaking, he coasted through seven innings as the Red Sox scored seven runs. Then he lay on a couch shivering under a blanket until his teammates burst in to celebrate. They were going to the World Series to face the New York Mets.

Boston won the Series opener, 1–0, at Shea Stadium behind Bruce Hurst. Clemens started Game 2; the Sox scored nine runs, but he didn't last long enough to get the 9–3 win.

The Series moved to Boston, where the Mets won the next two. Boston won Game 5, and the two teams went back to New York. Warming up for Game 6, Clemens realized that he had the chance to pitch the Red Sox to their first world championship since 1918. He had a 3–2 lead in the seventh when a pesky blister that had come up on his pitching hand tore open and began to bleed. He had to leave the game.

The Mets tied it in the eighth. They went into extra innings. When Boston scored two in the 10th and took a 5–3 lead, the clubhouse boys got ready to pop open the champagne. After the first two Mets flied out in the bottom of the 10th, the scoreboard flashed, "Congratulations, Boston Red Sox."

The Red Sox never got the third out. Three singles, a wild pitch, and a ground ball that went through the first baseman's legs gave the Mets the game and left Clemens and the Red Sox

*October 25, 1986, was the most disappointing day of Clemens's career. The Red Sox were one out away from winning their first World Series since 1918 when an error led to the Mets tying the score and going on to win the Series. Conferring on the mound in that ill-fated Game 6 are, from left, manager John McNamara, third baseman Wade Boggs, catcher Rich Gedman (No. 10), Clemens, and first baseman Bill Buckner.*

stunned and numb. They would have to play a seventh game.

It rained the next day, giving Clemens an extra day to do his running and ice his arm in case he was needed in the deciding game. He watched the whole game from the bullpen, hoping to get the call. The Red Sox used six pitchers trying to stave off defeat, but Clemens was not one of them. The Mets won, 8–5.

Clemens' 24–4 record earned him the Cy Young and Most Valuable Player Awards, plus a host of other honors, all of which he would have gladly traded for a World Series winner's ring. But he was only 24. His arm was healthy; there would be other opportunities.

The disappointing ending to his spectacular season was forgotten when his first son, Koby Aaron, was born on December 4. For Clemens, that was the best part of his personal highlight film.

During the season Clemens had noticed that by late August his legs felt weaker. He seemed to lose some velocity on his fastball. That winter he found a trainer in Houston who worked with him, adding inches to his legs and rump. He worked out on his old high school field, where he tied tires to a harness and dragged them behind him as he ran across the parking lot. Some of the high school players joined him.

It paid off. After a contract dispute cost him much of spring training and he got off to an erratic start, he finished the 1987 season strong with a 20–9 record and a career-high 18 complete games. He won his second straight Cy Young Award. But there was no World Series for the Red Sox that year.

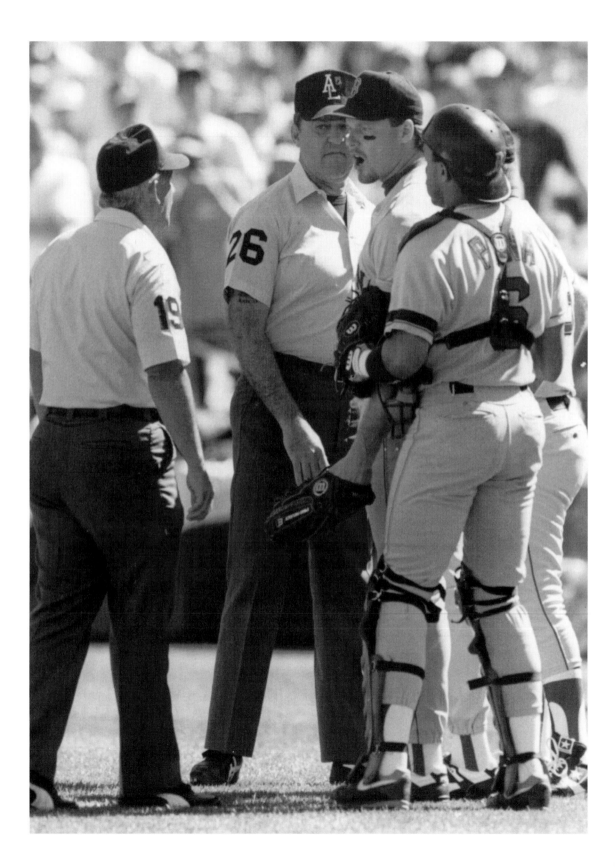

# 5

# THE CURSE OF THE BAMBINO

To Roger Clemens, pitching was combat. As one pitcher put it, "With him, it's not a game. It's WAR."

Catcher Rick Cerone got an early glimpse of Clemens' nasty streak. "It's the first game I ever caught him, April 19, 1988, in Detroit. I'm new to the team; he's a two-time Cy Young winner. First inning, the Detroit leadoff man singles. Next man up, Lou Whitaker, hits a home run. Next batter gets a hit. It's already 2–0, still nobody out. I'm thinking, 'What am I doing wrong?' Clemens' first pitch to the next batter sends him sprawling in the dirt. As he comes off the mound to take the throw back to him, he hollers loud enough for everybody to hear it, 'This is going to stop—now!'

"And it did. He wound up winning, 7–3."

The Red Sox won their second division title in three years. But the Oakland A's sent them home early, sweeping the four-game American League Championship Series (ALCS). For Roger, home now included another son, Kory Allen, born May 31.

Clemens started and finished the 1989 season strong, but in August he missed a few starts with tightness in his forearm and elbow. Throwing his fastballs put a tremendous strain on the muscles

*An outstanding 21–6 season in 1990 ended in frustration for Clemens when the Red Sox lost the ALCS to Oakland for the second time in three years. Clemens blew his top in the second inning of the final game and was ejected. Here he gets in a final shot at the umpires.*

of his arm and shoulder. He used more ice than a skating rink, often emptying the ice machines in hotels on the road to repair the damage done from his relentless "pounding" of the hitters.

The Red Sox finished a disappointing third in 1989.

Later, looking back at the 1990 season, Clemens told a writer he considered it "a tremendous year," even better than his first Cy Young season in 1986. He was 21–6 with a 1.93 ERA, his lowest ever. From late July through August he went 8–0 with an 0.80 ERA. In 67 innings he gave up only six runs and six walks while striking out 65.

Shoulder problems sidelined him for three weeks in September, probably costing him another Cy Young. The nagging ache and the forced idleness riled him. With a constant fire raging inside him, sometimes he boiled over. If he made a bad pitch he would yell at himself on the mound. If he threw too many of them and lost, chairs, tables, light bulbs, and doors might be destroyed. But sitting on the bench was the worst.

"Sometimes he forgets he's a human being," Bill Fischer said. "I have to remind him that even a pitching machine throws a bad one every once in a while. But if he wasn't that hard on himself, and didn't react that way, he wouldn't be the same pitcher, right up there with the best I've seen in over 50 years."

Somebody removed his name from his locker in Boston and replaced it with "Possessed Rebel." Roger loved it.

The Red Sox won the AL East in 1990 and once again faced Oakland for the chance to go to the World Series. The A's swaggered with confidence, having swept the Giants in the 1989 Series.

In the opener in Boston, Clemens opposed the A's ace, Dave Stewart. In five years Roger had never beaten Stewart, losing seven times to him. Clemens had won three Cy Young Awards, Stewart none. But Stewart had something Clemens wanted more than any trophies—a World Series ring.

Boston hadn't won a World Series since they had sold Babe Ruth to the Yankees 70 years earlier. That history dogged every Red Sox team. After their crushing defeat in 1986 and their loss to the A's in the '88 ALCS, the media never let them forget "The Curse of the Bambino."

"Believe me," Clemens told a reporter, "it's on my mind all the time."

Clemens shut out the A's for six innings, then left with a 1–0 lead when his lack of work caught up with him. The A's piled up the runs against the bullpen, winning 9–1.

On the bench in Game 2, Clemens never let up, ragging the A's and the umpires throughout Oakland's 4–1 victory. It got so vicious one of the A's, coming off the field, passed the Red Sox dugout and said, "Hey, what's the big deal?"

"The big deal," Clemens yelled, "is that we haven't won a World Series since 1918."

"Drink some milk and eat some bananas," the Oakland player said, meaning, "Calm down." But asking Roger Clemens to calm down was like trying to turn off lightning.

It got worse. In Oakland, after the A's won Game 3, Clemens's head of steam combined with frustration to form a volatile mix. On the afternoon of October 10 he watched the A's laughing and strutting, while their fans carried brooms in anticipation of the sweep.

*Fierce competitors like Oakland ace Dave Stewart and Roger Clemens believe that their aggressiveness comes from within themselves. "You can't teach us to be the people we are," said Stewart, who beat Clemens eight straight times over a five-year period.*

Clemens and Stewart squared off again. Neither team scored in the first. In the bottom of the second, two singles and an error put A's on second and third with one out. Mark McGwire's grounder to shortstop scored the first run. Willie Randolph was the next batter.

The count went to 3 and 0. Clemens kicked dirt around the mound, muttering to himself. He threw a fastball, high and inside. Umpire Terry Cooney called it a strike. Clemens threw another fastball in the same place. Cooney called it ball four.

Disgusted, Clemens swore loudly at himself. Cooney said something to him from behind home plate. Clemens jawed back, cursing and saying he was yelling at himself, not the umpire. The umpire thought the words were aimed at him. Cooney waved his arm and threw Clemens out of the game.

At first Clemens was unaware of what had happened. Second baseman Jody Reed went to the mound and said, "You've been thrown out of the game."

When he realized that he had been thumbed, Clemens ran toward Cooney, and the volcano really erupted.

Dave Stewart shut out the Red Sox until the ninth for the 3–1 clincher. The fans waved their brooms with glee. Clemens put on his black leather pants, gold western shirt, and boots, and went home.

The day after the Los Angeles Dodgers completed a World Series sweep of their own against the A's, Clemens ran three miles in the rain in Houston. Next season had begun.

In the spring of 1991 Clemens began working on a forkball or split-finger fastball. Thrown with the same motion as his fastball, it became a devastating pitch that broke down sharply just as the batter was about to make contact with it. Kirby Puckett said the pitch should be illegal, it was so hard to hit.

Clemens won his first four decisions, served the five-day suspension from his 1990 ALCS ejection, then won his fifth, retiring 24 of the last 27 White Sox batters. Later he ran off another six wins in a row, and finished with an 18–10 record and a league-leading 2.63 ERA and four shutouts. Three times he left a game with the lead, only to have the bullpen lose it. His 271 innings pitched was the second highest work-load of his career. It all earned him his third Cy Young Award.

For the next four years, Clemens averaged only 10 wins a year. His '93 and '95 seasons were interrupted by extended time on the disabled list with a sore elbow and strained muscle behind his right shoulder. In '95 he failed to pitch a complete game for the first time.

His declining win totals and increasing DL time put Boston officials in a quandary when he finished the 1996 season with a 10–13 record. Despite his workload of 242 innings, they pondered the wear and tear on his 34-year-old shoulder, and the amount of money it would take to re-sign him.

Pitcher Jamie Moyer observed, "He was at the end of his contract and he wanted to stay in Boston. But it didn't look like Boston was going to honor that. Roger gave great efforts outing after outing. We didn't score any runs for him when he pitched. He never opened his mouth, never complained. He kept working despite the losses."

If it were up to the players in the Red Sox clubhouse, they would have said, "Sign him."

*Clemens works on his fielding as much as any other part of his game. He has not made more than two errors in a season in the past 10 years.*

The fans, opposing hitters, umpires, and the press knew the short-tempered, mean, nasty, sometimes surly Roger Clemens. One player said, "He struts around out there like . . . I'm Roger God Clemens and nobody's going to hit me."

That image was just fine with Clemens. He wanted to come across that way when he was in his office on the mound. But in the clubhouse, the man behind the glare and the high hard one was admired and respected.

Jamie Moyer noticed, "When Roger pitches, people play for him. There's a little more effort, intensity, and concentration behind him."

Infielder John Valentin confirmed it. "As a rookie I was really nervous playing behind him, not wanting to drop any balls when he pitched. He took care of the young players and supported us. If you had any questions or needed help on or off the field, you could look to him."

First baseman Mo Vaughn said, "He taught me everything about what it takes to be successful in this game. His attitude of hard work rubbed off on me. You watch the way he walks into the clubhouse, how he takes the mound and goes about his business, how he handles success and admits his faults."

Catcher Bill Haselman illustrated what it meant to the rest of the team to have Clemens on the mound. "It was late in a close game. There were a couple guys on base. The manager came out to the mound and said, 'How do you feel?' Roger looked a little tired.

"Mo Vaughn came over from first base. 'Stay in there, man,' Mo said. 'We need you to finish out this inning. Let's go.'

"That was all Roger needed. He just nodded, but I know he was thinking, 'I'll finish it, no matter how tired I am.' And he did."

"I would tell him to stay in there," Vaughn added, "because even at 75 or 80 percent he was better than anybody else. He has the heart of a lion and is a true competitor in every situation."

In the dugout, Clemens was the head cheerleader. He liked to chatter, riding the umpires or the other team. He was the first to give a pat on the back, or to boost a guy who was down with an encouraging word.

If another pitcher asked him a question, he would get all the help he wanted. Clemens advised the young pitchers to put their work first and say no to anything, like interviews, that cut into their work time.

Aaron Sele recalled, "If you decided to slow down your work habits and your pitching started slipping and hurting the team, he'd say, 'Hey, you need to get back to work.' He was the real leader of the pitchers."

Clemens tried to inoculate the young pitchers with his confidence and willpower. "You see a lot of guys who lack confidence and are afraid to lose. It's difficult when you're a starter and you pitch poorly; there's so much down time between starts. If I pitch poorly I increase my work and try to punish myself just to get it out of my mind.

"Every time you think of something negative, try to replace it with 10 positives."

Despite all his glaring and complaining, umpires enjoyed working behind the plate when Clemens pitched because he threw strikes. Tim McClelland said, "Umpires want a pitcher who's always around the plate. Clemens has always been a pleasure to work."

The public and media never saw the funny side of Clemens. "No one knows this about him, but he's one of the funniest guys around," said Mo Vaughn. "Until it's time for work, then it stops. Even then, here's this 6' 4", 235-pound intense competitor giving you these one-liners. He has a different way of putting things. He'd holler over to me and second baseman Jeff Frye, 'Keep it airtight over there.' When certain lefties came up to bat, he'd tell me to play way back to get everything I could, and he'd cover first base and 'we'll cancel Christmas,' meaning we'll shut the other team down."

On the bus, in the dugout and clubhouse, he was quick with a teasing jab, swapping zingers, keeping everybody around him laughing. Pitching coach Bill Fischer was the butt of one of Roger's jokes. "When he's not pitching, Roger is the life of the bench, the court jester. I had a hard time hearing the phone ring in the dugout. He picked up on that. He'd say, 'Hey, Fish, the phone's ringing,' when it wasn't. I'd run over to answer it and there was nobody there."

Players were awed by his workouts. Nobody tried to keep up with him. "There was a machine in the clubhouse called the versaclimber," said Rick Cerone. "You stand on it pumping your arms and legs like you're climbing a hill. I would get on there and do maybe 15 minutes. He'd go on it for an hour and a half, sweat pouring off him."

When Clemens went home to Katy after the 1996 season and it looked like he wouldn't be coming back to Boston, Aaron Sele said, "All the pitchers were saddened to see him go. He was our leader; he ran the show. You felt like you lost a friend."

In his 13 seasons in Boston, Clemens had won 192 and lost 111 with a 3.06 ERA. His strikeouts-to-walks ratio was 3:1. But that was all in the past. The Red Sox were reluctant to guarantee more than two years to a 34-year-old pitcher with a fragile shoulder.

Clemens was confident that he could last more than two years and still carry a full work-load and win. "I've always been doubted and I've always responded. If somebody says I can't do something, I've got to show him he's wrong."

# 6

# GODZILLA ON THE HILL

Once they became convinced that Roger Clemens was not returning to Boston, a dozen teams began bidding for him. Some sent private jets to fly him to their cities. Others came to Katy to see him. He argued with himself for days over whether to accept less to stay in Boston. But the difference became too great to ignore.

Criticized for being greedy, Clemens bristled. "I've worked to keep myself in an elite group. Whatever the going rate is, that's what I'm going to make. When you win the lottery, you're a hero. But when you work your butt off to earn a million dollars, you're not."

On December 13, 1996, he signed with the Toronto Blue Jays, who guaranteed him three years with an option for the year 2000. Equally important, they welcomed his two oldest boys, Koby and Kory, to practice in the SkyDome before games and gave them their own uniforms and lockers.

Having his sons in the clubhouse with him reminded him of the loss of his stepfather when he was nine. "I saw my teammates' fathers come in the clubhouse to visit them and I was jealous," he told a writer. "I still miss my dad's not enjoying

*Clemens has a hug for first baseman Mo Vaughn after the Red Sox clinched the AL East in 1995. Vaughn, the league's MVP that year, said Clemens "taught me everything about what it takes to be successful in this game."*

my success. I used to see Mo Vaughn's dad in the clubhouse, celebrating with him and hugging him after hitting a home run. I tell players how lucky they are. I don't have that."

Clemens took the whole family to spring training in Dunedin, Florida; there were now four Clemens boys: Kacy Austin, born July 27, 1994, and Kody Alec, born May 15, 1996, in addition to Koby and Kory.

In the Blue Jays clubhouse Clemens found his number 21 being worn by 24-year-old Carlos Delgado, who surrendered it to him without hesitating. Later Clemens thanked him with an expensive Rolex watch, which prompted pitcher Paul Quantrill to ask, "Do you want my number 48 too?"

Clemens immediately became the leader on his new team. "He was the man who would go to the guy who had a bad day and say something to buck him up," said manager Tim Johnson. "He was always talking to other players in the clubhouse, with a lot of kidding, and appreciation of the players behind him on the field. Players went to him for advice in anything on or off the field."

Slugger Jose Canseco and Clemens became inseparable pals and sparring partners in the weight room and clubhouse.

Clemens lost no time showing up his doubters. Durwood Merrill, a Texan who had been an umpire for 21 years, wrote, "Even though he turned 35 . . . the man was Godzilla on the hill in '97. . . . The glare was back. Baseball relearned a great lesson about Clemens: pitching, regardless of your physical state, is still a matter of energizing your attitude."

Don Zimmer, a baseball man for more than 50 years, said, "Clemens was more dominating in '97 than at any time in his career because he had more pitches." Clemens would throw any of his six pitches on any count in any situation.

Clemens won his first 11 decisions and finished with a 21–7 record. The first pitcher in more than 50 years to lead the league in wins, ERA (2.05), and strikeouts (292), he won his fourth Cy Young Award. But the Blue Jays, last in hitting, finished fifth.

On the road Clemens was not one to sit in a hotel room watching television. He enjoyed playing golf and going sightseeing. He was as fiercely competitive on the golf course as he was on the mound. "But once the game was over," Rick Cerone said, "he was a good, warmhearted person. After the season, he'd send everybody who played golf with him a gold money clip like the PGA one, engraved 'Member of the Mini-tour.'"

After 15 years, Clemens was as close to unhittable in 1998 as he had been as a rookie in the Eastern League. After a loss to Cleveland on May 29, he reeled off 15 straight wins. He needed one more to tie the league record for consecutive wins, but in his last start it took 13 innings before the Jays defeated the Detroit Tigers 5–4. Toronto had won every one of his last 22 starts.

Midway through the season he said, "I've had a lot of individual success in my career. I could win 20 games this year and get a handshake and a pat on the back and go home and watch the playoffs, so to me it's meaningless. I don't care if you get 20 wins or hit .350; it does no good unless you're winning."

Clemens got 20 wins against six losses, with a 2.65 ERA. But the Blue Jays finished four games back of the Red Sox for the wild card spot in the playoffs. The place reserved for the World

*Clemens wears the same game face whether he's getting beat or throwing a shutout, batter after batter. When he throws his 97-mph heater, hitters have four-tenths of a second to react. That's less time than it takes to blink your eyes.*

Series ring in the Clemens trophy case remained empty. But he added another Cy Young award, becoming the first pitcher to win five. His mission had been to win one for each of his four sons. "Now, Dad," they told him, "you have one for yourself."

Celebrity comes with a price tag. Stars are pulled in all directions by people wanting a piece of their time or money or fame. If they are recognized in public, all hopes for privacy disappear. There was no way Roger Clemens could stroll through a mall looking in store windows, or eat in a restaurant without being pestered for autographs.

It was impossible for him to fulfill all the demands on his time, but Clemens was active in several Red Sox charities during his 13 years in

Boston. Many times while running through the streets around Fenway after batting practice, he would drop in at one of the nearby children's hospitals. "I really got the 'Christmas-eyes' looks when I showed up in uniform, more so than in street clothes. Being able to make someone happy like that is truly exciting. Baseball players have a rare opportunity to do something for society . . . If a ballplayer ignores a last-wish kid, he's abusing his privilege."

Before heading to spring training each year, Clemens helped coach his sons' Little League teams and went to their games whenever his team was in Texas. But that was another area where being a star got in the way of being a dad.

"It's a fiasco when I show up at one of their games. I try to creep into the stands, but as soon as somebody sees me, they start yelling at their kids to play harder, as if I can sign them. And the parents don't leave me alone. I have to leave my wife and her mom and take my four-year-old and go sit on the bench.

"And when my kids come up to bat, people think they're nine going on 20 and should be more than they are. I have to remind people they're just boys. I imagine as time goes on my

*Clemens values time with his family above everything else when he is not pitching. The Blue Jays' willingness to allow his two oldest boys, Kory (left) and Koby, to work out with him in the Sky-Dome was one factor in his signing with Toronto after the 1996 season.*

kids will have a little extra pressure on them if they're still playing."

Clemens puts no pressure on them as a coach or father. "Win or lose, I try to make it as much fun for them as I can. But they put pressure on themselves. They try so hard to impress me the few times I'm there, I have to tell them if they're hustling all the time they are on the field, that's great with me."

Like dads everywhere, he learned that the same advice coming from somebody else often carried more weight than when he said it. "I've been telling them for five years how to grip the bat to hit the top half of the ball and finish through. Then they go to Jose Canseco and he tells them the same thing. Next thing you know they're doing it. They say to me, 'Canseco told me to do this, dad.' And I'll just say, 'That's great.'"

To other parents and coaches, Clemens was a star pitcher headed for the Hall of Fame. But to his kids he was just dad. And that suited him perfectly.

"When I was with the Red Sox and we had a house in Framingham, about 20 miles from Fenway, I'd be sitting there eating breakfast in the morning and I'd hear the door open. I look up and there's 20 of the neighborhood kids looking at me. Koby, who was nine, would say, 'Okay, guys, there he is. I told you my dad was Roger Clemens. Now let's go play.' And they'd go play. And when they chose up teams Koby'd rather be Mo Vaughn than the Rocket."

Clemens was happy to share any tips he gave his own boys and their teams with anyone who asked.

"I taught them from the git-go good mechanics in throwing from any position. Kids get tired. They can't throw for long if they don't use proper mechanics. Throwing from the outfield is like Robin Hood shooting an arrow. Keep the front shoulder closed, so it doesn't fly open.

"When they play catch I try to get them to get their push-off leg into a slot, which means turn it sideways. If both your feet are pointing to the kid you're throwing to, your shoulder's going to come right open."

His own experience with pitching coaches taught Clemens the importance of finding the right word or phrase that will click with a youngster and help him remember it down the road. "Everything I tell one person about pitching or throwing might not click with them. All I can do is try and hope it clicks. Sometimes another coach might say the right thing that does click.

"With kids you have to recognize that some are more easily intimidated, more afraid of making mistakes. They won't come out of their shell as much. Others are very aggressive. Some I can get on and challenge them and they'll sit up and show you. Others may go the other direction."

Clemens suggested that parents write notes about their kids for the coaches: "the position the kid enjoys most; what aspect of character they would like to see the kid improve in."

On pitching, Clemens had this to say:

"I wouldn't suggest any youngster start throwing breaking balls until he's a very mature 12-year-old, and then only some type of slurve (slider-curve). Ten is too young. Kids are always asking me how to throw a forkball or knuckleball or curve. I show them the two different fastballs and ask them if they can throw them to nine different areas of the strike zone. Most of them can't do it. I think a good fastball and a

*Before going to spring training each year, Clemens helps coach his sons' Little League teams in Texas. After the 1998 Little League World Series, he invited Jeff Duda, the Series pitching star from Langley, British Columbia, to visit him in the Toronto dugout on August 30.*

pretty good changeup at that level can do a lot of good."

Clemens finished the 1998 season with 233 career wins. If he never won another game, he was already measured for a place in the Hall of Fame. As for going for 300 wins, the pitchers' equivalent of 3,000 hits, Clemens said he would leave that up to his family. Fiercely protective of their welfare and privacy, and conscious of his obligations to them, he recalled one scene that has stuck in his mind.

"In 1993 the Red Sox flew me to Texas for Nolan Ryan's retirement day. Ryan was giving his speech and his two boys were standing behind him. One of them was midway through college and the other was on his way into college. You knew Ryan had missed a lot of things that they had done along the way.

"I stood there and vowed, 'I'm not going to be away from my boys that long.'

"What I do after 2000 is up to my family. They've sacrificed a lot for me to do what I wanted to do. I don't know what they'll say. One week I get from the two oldest boys: 'Dad, when are you going to retire?' Ten days later they're asking me if I'm going to go for 300 wins. We'll just have to wait and see."

Clemens, 36, had two goals that were more important to him: winning that elusive World Series ring, and pitching for the United States in the 2000 Olympics in Australia. "It seems far-fetched, but I'd like to play for my country and win a medal. I'd like for that to be my last stop."

Clemens's chances of reaching his World Series goal soared when the rebuilding Blue Jays, acceding to his wish to be traded to a contender, dealt Clemens to the defending world champion New York Yankees just as spring training began in February 1999.

"I know the tradition in New York," Clemens said when told of the trade. "I love pitching in Yankee Stadium, and all the stuff that goes with it. It's part of history."

The five-time Cy Young winner is also part of history, "A nonstop Hall of Famer," said Yankees manager Joe Torre.

# CHRONOLOGY

1962    Born in Dayton, Ohio, August 4.

1976    Family moves to Texas.

1981    Drafted by New York Mets.
        Enrolls at University of Texas.

1983    Wins College World Series final for University of Texas.
        Signs with Boston Red Sox.

1984    Gets first major league win, 5–4, at Minnesota May 16.
        Marries Debbie Godfrey.

1986    Strikes out major league record 20 Seattle Mariners
            without walking a batter April 29.
        Winning pitcher and MVP of All-Star Game.
        Wins first of four Cy Young Awards.
        First of four sons, Koby Aaron, born December 4.

1996    Ties Cy Young's Red Sox record of 192 wins and
            38 shutouts September 18.
        Signs with Toronto Blue Jays December 13.

1997    Wins fourth Cy Young Award.

1998    Becomes first pitcher to win five Cy Young awards.

1999    Traded to New York Yankees in February.

# STATISTICS

## BOSTON RED SOX, TORONTO BLUE JAYS

| Year | Team | W | L | ERA | G | GS | CG | IP | H | BB | SO | SHO |
|------|------|---|---|-----|---|----|----|-----|---|----|----|-----|
| 1984 | BOS A | 9 | 4 | 4.32 | 21 | 20 | 5 | 133.1 | 146 | 29 | 126 | 1 |
| 1985 | | 7 | 5 | 3.29 | 15 | 15 | 3 | 98.1 | 83 | 37 | 74 | 1 |
| 1986 | | 24 | 4 | 2.48 | 33 | 33 | 10 | 254 | 179 | 67 | 238 | 1 |
| 1987 | | 20 | 9 | 2.97 | 36 | 36 | 18 | 281.2 | 248 | 83 | 256 | 7 |
| 1988 | | 18 | 12 | 2.93 | 35 | 35 | 14 | 264 | 217 | 62 | 291 | 8 |
| 1989 | | 17 | 11 | 3.13 | 35 | 35 | 8 | 253.1 | 215 | 93 | 230 | 3 |
| 1990 | | 21 | 6 | 1.93 | 31 | 31 | 7 | 228.1 | 193 | 54 | 209 | 4 |
| 1991 | | 18 | 10 | 2.62 | 35 | 35 | 13 | 271.1 | 219 | 65 | 241 | 4 |
| 1992 | | 18 | 11 | 2.41 | 32 | 32 | 11 | 246.2 | 203 | 62 | 208 | 5 |
| 1993 | | 11 | 14 | 4.46 | 29 | 29 | 2 | 191.2 | 170 | 67 | 160 | 1 |
| 1994 | | 9 | 7 | 2.85 | 24 | 24 | 3 | 170.2 | 124 | 71 | 168 | 1 |
| 1995 | | 10 | 5 | 4.18 | 23 | 23 | 0 | 140 | 141 | 60 | 132 | 0 |
| 1996 | | 10 | 13 | 3.63 | 34 | 34 | 6 | 242.2 | 216 | 106 | 257 | 2 |
| 1997 | TOR A | 21 | 7 | 2.05 | 34 | 34 | 9 | 264 | 204 | 68 | 292 | 3 |
| 1998 | | 20 | 6 | 2.65 | 33 | 33 | 5 | 234.2 | 169 | 88 | 271 | 3 |
| **Totals** | | **233** | **124** | **2.97** | **450** | **449** | **114** | **3238.2** | **2732** | **1012** | **3153** | **44** |

**World Series**

| Year | Team | W | L | ERA | G | GS | CG | IP | H | BB | SO | SHO |
|------|------|---|---|-----|---|----|----|-----|---|----|----|-----|
| 1986 | | 0 | 0 | 3.18 | 2 | 2 | 0 | 11.1 | 9 | 6 | 11 | 0 |

# FURTHER READING

Clemens, Roger. *Rocket Man.* Boston: S. Greene Press, 1987.

Devaney, John. *Sports Great Roger Clemens.* Springfield, N.J.: Enslow Publishers, 1990.

Shaughnessy, Dan. *Curse of the Bambino.* New York: Viking Penguin, 1991.

Weber, Bruce. *Baseball Megastars.* New York: Scholastic, 1998.

Young, Ken. *Cy Young Award Winners.* New York: Walker & Co., 1994.

# INDEX

---

PICTURE CREDITS

AP/Wide World Photos: pp. 8, 22, 27, 30, 33, 36, 38, 42, 44, 48, 52, 53, 56, 58; Courtesy of Boston Red Sox: p. 2; Courtesy of Charles Maiorana: pp. 14, 18; Rice University Athletic News Bureau: p. 20; Transcendental Graphics: pp. 11, 32

NORMAN L. MACHT is the author of more than 25 books, 20 of them for Chelsea House Publishers. He is also the coauthor of biographies of former ballplayers Dick Bartell and Rex Barney, and is a member of the Society for American Baseball Research. He is the president of Choptank Syndicate, Inc. and lives in Easton, Maryland.

JIM MURRAY, who passed away in 1998, was a veteran sports columnist of the *Los Angeles Times*, and one of America's most acclaimed writers. He was named "America's Best Sportswriter" by the National Association of Sportscasters and Sportswriters 14 times, was awarded the Red Smith Award, and was twice winner of the National Headliner Award. In addition, he was awarded the J. G. Taylor Spink Award in 1987 for "meritorious contributions to baseball writing." With this award came his 1988 induction into the National Baseball Hall of Fame in Cooperstown, New York. In 1990, Jim Murray was awarded the Pulitzer Prize for Commentary.

EARL WEAVER is the winningest manager in the Baltimore Orioles' history by a wide margin. He compiled 1,480 victories in his 17 years at the helm. After managing eight different minor league teams, he was given the chance to lead the Orioles in 1968. Under his leadership the Orioles finished lower than second place in the American League East only four times in 17 years. One of only 12 managers in big league history to have managed in four or more World Series, Earl was named Manager of the Year in 1979. The popular Weaver had his number, 5, retired in 1982, joining Brooks Robinson, Frank Robinson, and Jim Palmer, whose numbers were retired previously. Earl Weaver continues his association with the professional baseball scene by writing, broadcasting, and coaching.